GEARED FOR GROWTH BIBLE STUDIES

BORN TO BE FREE

A STUDY IN GALATIANS

BIBLE STUDIES TO IMPACT THE LIVES OF ORDINARY PEOPLE

Written by Marie Dinnen

The Word Worldwide

CHRISTIAN FOCUS

For details of our titles visit us on our website
www.christianfocus.com

ISBN 1-84550-019-9

10 9 8 7 6 5 4 3 2 1

Published in 2005 by
Christian Focus Publications Ltd, Geanies House,
Fearn, Tain, Ross-shire, IV20 ITW, Scotland
and
WEC International, Bulstrode, Oxford Road,
Gerrards Cross, Bucks, SL9 8SZ

Cover design by Alister MacInnes

Printed and bound by Bell & Bain, Glasgow

CONTENTS

QUESTIONS AND NOTES

ANSWER GUIDE

PREFACE
GEARED FOR GROWTH

'Where there's LIFE there's GROWTH:
Where there's GROWTH there's LIFE.'

WHY GROW a study group?

Because as we study the Bible and share together we can

- learn to combat loneliness, depression, staleness, frustration, and other problems
- get to understand and love each other
- become responsive to the Holy Spirit's dealing and obedient to God's Word

and that's GROWTH.

How do you GROW a study group?

- Just start by asking a friend to join you and then aim at expanding your group.
- Study the set portions daily (they are brief and easy: no catches).
- Meet once a week to discuss what you find.
- Befriend others, both Christians and non-Christians, and work away together

see how it GROWS!

WHEN you GROW ...

This will happen at school, at home, at work, at play, in your youth group, your student fellowship, women's meetings, mid-week meetings, churches and communities,

you'll be REACHING THROUGH TEACHING.

INTRODUCTORY STUDY

PLAY: TRADITION OR TRUTH?

Scene: Jerusalem TV Studio I. About 40 AD.

Characters: Announcer; Jewish Priest; Jewish business man; King Agrippa; Greek Chemist; European Christian convert; Paul of Tarsus.

Announcer: '... that is the end of the news and weather forecast for today. However, aware of the controversy which has been stirred up over the claims made by Paul of Tarsus, JTV I is introducing tonight the first of a series of interviews on the subject. Paul claims he has had a recent encounter with Jesus Christ. He maintains that Jesus is indeed the long awaited Messiah and that this revelation has revolutionised his whole way of life and thinking. It is now seven years since the crucifixion of Jesus and we thought all the rumours and fantasies about His being alive had died down, but here they are; the old arguments are at boiling point again.'

Ist Interview 'Tonight we introduce to you an authority on the subject, Rabban Gamaliel, representing the school of Hillel, a wing of the Pharisees. Paul studied under him and therefore he speaks from firsthand knowledge of the man. Rabban, can you throw light on Paul's present convictions?'

Rabban Gamaliel 'Paul is a most able scholar. He is held in very high regard by both his teachers and fellow students. He has been actively engaged under our directive, in seeking to stamp out this Jesus movement which cuts right across our teaching. Paul is most devout in his keeping of the law and upholding our Jewish rites and traditions. I can only conclude that there has been a grave accusation made against Paul. The rumours must be false or Paul has gone insane.'

2nd Interview '... and tonight to continue our series on Paul and Jesus, we have a Jewish business man, Mr A. Benjamin, Director of Golddiggers Incorporated. Thank you, Mr Benjamin; Can you state your views on Paul's claims?

Mr A. Benjamin 'Well, there's very little I can say. He must have become mentally unbalanced. He's a fellow who should know better than to say such way-out things. Like me, his family brought him up a good Jew. He's educated way beyond my level and we all respect him very much. But I think he's really flipped to say Jesus is alive. We Jews know the Messiah will come, but he will come like a king in mighty power. It is utterly ridiculous for Paul to line up with those who tried to make that fellow Jesus our Messiah. Why, we saw Him die between two thieves. The whole thing is utter nonsense.'

3rd Interview

Announcer: 'Our first two interviews concerning Paul and Jesus left us with the impression that Paul has in some way been misjudged. Since starting this series we have heard that Paul has been put to official trial. Tonight we have the very person who handled his case. Ladies and gentlemen, I present to you King Agrippa himself. Your Royal Highness, did your handling of Paul result from these declarations being made about him?'

K. Agrippa: 'Yes indeed. Certain Jews accused Paul to Festus, Procurator of Judaea. They maintained that his teachings not only undermined all that the Jewish law and temple stand for, but that he was even a threat to my position and government. Paul, as a Roman citizen, appealed to me to judge the matter and I agreed to do so.'

Announcer: 'And what did you find, Your Highness?'

K. Agrippa: 'Festus thought Paul's story so fantastic that he accused him of being insane. However, I assessed him to be giving a truthful and unexaggerated account of what happened to him. He is absolutely convinced that the resurrection of Christ is according to the Jewish prophets. He spoke with such conviction and authority that even I was almost persuaded towards his point of view and felt he should go free.'

Announcer: 'Your Royal Highness, thank you for appearing on JTV I tonight and for your valuable contribution to this series.'

4th Interview

Announcer: 'For tonight's interview in the Paul and Jesus series we have sought a spokesman who could take a completely neutral position regarding this controversial topic. Mr. Pharmakos, would you care to introduce yourself to our viewers?'

Mr. Pharmakos:	'Thank you. I am a chemist and run my business in Main Street, Jerusalem.'
Announcer:	'Have you always resided there?'
Mr. Pharmakos:	'No, my family came originally from Ephesus.'
Announcer:	'You do not then identify with the Jewish religion?'
Mr. Pharmakos:	'No, I find their law and customs quite different from mine. Our family worships the Virgin Goddess, Diana and we belonged to the Artemis Temple in Ephesus. We are not familiar with Yahweh, the God of Israel.'
Announcer:	'Have you formed any opinion of this Jew, Paul, who claims to have met the Jews' Messiah?'
Mr. Pharmakos:	'Well, I think he's a bit of a crank myself. A couple of Jews came into my shop the other day and we were discussing the matter together. One felt Paul was quite wrong and should get back to his traditional views on the laws and rites of Israel. The other thought Paul was right and that it was possible to accept Paul's teaching and keep the Jewish laws and feasts as well. There seems to be confusion as to whether the Jews are now to worship their Yahweh or Jesus. Must admit, although they tried to persuade me to one opinion or the other, that the whole thing is a jigsaw puzzle to me. I'd rather stick to my own religion.'

5th Interview

Announcer:	'This will be the last in our series unless we can get hold of Paul himself to talk to us. Tonight we have a woman to interview. I now introduce to you Madame Lydia of Thyatira. Madame Lydia, when and where did you meet Paul of Tarsus?'
Madame Lydia:	'I met him at Philippi where I am an overseas agent of the Purple Goods Company of Thyatira.'
Announcer:	'Was Paul then interested in your wares?'
Madame Lydia:	'No, in Thyatira I had been associated with a group of Jews because I wanted to learn about their faith. When I went to Philippi I sought out some Jews there and used to gather with them by the river each Sabbath.

We were worshipping Yahweh there one day when Paul found us and started to tell us of his encounter with the Risen Christ.'

Announcer: 'Did you believe him?'

Madame Lydia: 'Most certainly. I knew immediately that Paul was speaking the truth. His teaching satisfied the longing of my heart to know God. After hearing more of Paul's teaching I accepted Jesus as the Christ, my Saviour. I and my household were baptised in the Christian faith.'

Announcer: 'So you would not consider Paul a crank?'

Madame Lydia: 'No. My faith in Christ is real through Paul's witness and I know he has been commissioned of God to spread the gospel far and wide.'

Announcer: 'Thank you, Lydia, for travelling so far to be with us tonight. I am sure your testimony to the authority of Paul's message will be most enlightening to our viewers.'

6th Interview

Announcer: 'Ladies and gentlemen, we are excited to be able to present to you tonight Paul of Tarsus himself. Now you will be left in no doubt as to what Paul really believes. You will have to decide for yourselves whether Paul is completely deceived or whether, as he claims, he comes to you with a message from God. Paul, can you tell us a little about yourself first?'

Paul: 'I was born a Roman in the city of Tarsus, but I come from the tribe of Benjamin and was educated under Jewish teachers. I am a Pharisee and a member of the Jewish Sanhedrin.'

Announcer: 'Do you still hold this role?'

Paul: 'I did until a short time ago. Under the direction of the Sanhedrin I was authorised to go and destroy the followers of Jesus who questioned our authority and the validity of the Mosaic law. However, as I was on my way to Damascus to wreak vengeance on those Christians, a most amazing thing happened to me. I encountered Jesus Christ Himself. I realised that I was absolutely mistaken in my convictions and very wrong in my actions. I discovered that Jesus is indeed the Christ, the Messiah, the

Son of the Living God. Since then I have set myself to study the Scriptures afresh and have come to this conclusion: Jesus is the One of whom our Prophets spoke.'

Announcer.   'This conviction has then changed your whole outlook on life, Paul?'

Paul: 'It most certainly has. Since my salvation is totally dependent upon Jesus alone, all the things I used to value most and felt put me in good standing with God, seem utterly worthless. My background, education, position in the Sanhedrin, zeal for the Jewish law and concept of myself being a 'good' Jew, have all gone by the board. "I suffer the loss of all things and count them but dung that I might win Christ, being found in Him, not clothed in my own self-righteousness which pertains to the law, but righteousness through faith in Christ alone . . . that I may know Him; the power of his resurrection, the fellowship of His suffering, being made conformable unto His death ... that I might attain to the resurrection."'

Announcer.   'Ladies and Gentlemen. You have heard Paul of Tarsus. The decision is now over to you. Is Paul mad? Or has he presented the truth of God? I leave the decision with you ...'

ABOUT *GALATIANS*

The little playlet gives us an impression of the controversies which arose when Paul firmly converted to Christ, took up his commission from God (Acts 9:15) and started to preach salvation through faith in Christ. Paul and Barnabas toured through Galatia with this message and churches were established (Acts 13) and revisited (Acts 14) that converts might be further consolidated in their faith. However, 'Judaizers' followed hot on Paul's heels (Acts 15) and said that the converts must also observe the Jewish laws and ceremonies (including rites like circumcision) and brought confusion on the young Christians.

He sends a personal letter to them, showing his deep burden for their spiritual well-being (2 Cor. 11:28) and his desire to see them grounded solidly in the truth that faith in *Christ* alone is essential to salvation. Later the church in Jerusalem took action when they received Paul's report on the Judaizers (Acts 15:20-32) and representatives, including Paul, were sent back to further teach and rid the church of this error.

STUDY 1
PAUL'S GOD-GLORIFYING GOSPEL

QUESTIONS

DAY 1 *Galatians 1:1-9.*
From these nine verses can you discover:
a) Who wrote this letter?

b) How does he describe himself?

c) To whom was he writing?

d) Why was he writing?

DAY 2 *Galatians 1:1.*
a) What major point about himself does Paul seem to be pressing home?

b) What other important truth does he refer to (Rom. 1:3-4)?

DAY 3 *Galatians 1:3-6.*
a) How does Paul identify with these believers?

b) What do the words 'grace' and 'peace' mean (Eph. 2:4-5; Col. 1:20-22)?

QUESTIONS (contd.)

DAY 4 *Galatians 1:3-4.*
a) What does it mean that Christ 'gave himself'?

b) What other things are said about His death in verse 4?

DAY 5 *Galatians 1:3-5.*
a) Does God wait till we are 'good' enough to offer us salvation (Titus 3:4-5a)?

b) How did Paul react when he thought about salvation and the death of Christ (v. 5)?

DAY 6 *Galatians 1:6-8.*
a) Whose gospel did Paul preach? Did he believe there were many ways to heaven?

b) Why was Paul concerned for these converts?

DAY 7 *Galatians 1:9-10.*
a) Why would Paul emphasise that he was not a man-pleaser?

b) How is the gospel summarised in I Corinthians 15:1-7?

Memory Verse: Galatians 1:9.

NOTES

STRAIGHT TO THE POINT

News of the Galatians being swayed by false teachers must have been a grief to Paul. Paul had preached that the only way to salvation was through faith in Christ's substitutionary death on the cross and in that alone. The Judaizers were saying: 'Oh, that's alright. But to be a good Christian you must also keep the old Jewish law, the rite of circumcision, etc., etc.'

Paul's answer to this situation came back as clear and loud. It can be summed up under four headings:

1. *Christ's commissioning to Paul*

Just as God invested Moses with His authority when he had to plead Israel's cause before Pharaoh (Exod. chs. 3 and 4) and the disciples when they were sent into the world as His ambassadors (Matt. 28:16-20), so Paul had been invested with His commissioning and authority (Acts 9:15). On CHRIST'S authority alone Paul came to the Galatians.

2. *Christ's message through Paul*

Christ gave Himself (Rom. 5:6-9).

According to His Father's will (Matt. 26:39 and Rev. 13:8).

That we might be released from our sins (Rom. 5:1).

And delivered from this evil environment (John 16:33).

Paul's teaching was firmly based on this *message alone*: faith in the resurrected Christ and His finished work of redemption.

3. *Other gospels*

The Judaizers were using Paul's message as a basis for their teaching, but adding extras. These extras would please legalistic Jews who self-righteously wanted to keep to the old Jewish laws and traditions. But such teaching could only bring judgment on their heads, Paul maintained. Their message of faith and works could only nullify the death of Christ. It was 'ANATHEMA', incurring the wrath of God, as did Achan in Joshua 7:19-21.

We need to remind ourselves that Satan is the father of lies (John 8:44) and has his host of lying demons who work through people, yes, even religious people to pervert the truth of God. Satan can transform himself into an angel of light (2 Cor. 11:14).

4. *Paul's Gospel*

The Judaizers had no doubt accused Paul of being a man-pleaser. However, verse 10 doesn't sound as though he was guilty of this. Read Acts 14:1-20.

Paul suffered so much for the gospel. Would he have done it just to please men? Not at all. Paul's one desire was to be a true bondservant of Christ (v. 10) and to glorify God (v. 5). This portion must surely cause us all to search our motives. What is our goal in life?

Above all, do we want to be true to Christ? Do we live our lives to please ourselves, or others, or God?

> So faith bounds forward to its goal in God
> And love can trust her Lord to lead her there ...
> One thing I *know*, I cannot say Him nay,
> One thing I *do*, I press towards my Lord;
> My God my glory here, from day to day.
> And in the glory there my great Reward.

STUDY 2
A SINGLE EYE FOR GOD'S GLORY

QUESTIONS

DAY 1   *Galatians 1:11-12; Acts 9:3-6; Matthew 16:13-17.*
a) What is unique to the gospel (v. 11)?

b) Why should we believe what Paul teaches about the gospel? In what way was Paul's grasp of truth similar to Peter's (Matt. 16:15-17)?

DAY 2   *Galatians 1:13-14; Philippians 3:4-6.*
a) What was Paul like before he met the Lord Jesus Christ?

b) What did his zeal drive him to do (see also v. 23)?

DAY 3   *Galatians 1:15-16.*
a) To what does Paul owe his conversion experience?

b) What was God's plan for Paul's life (Acts 26:16-19)? How did he respond to this?

DAY 4   *Galatians 1:15-16.*
a) 'Christianity is not about rules or a ritual, but a relationship with another Person.' Would Paul have agreed with this statement?

b) Did Paul ever regret becoming a Christian (2:20b; Phil. 3:7-8)?

QUESTIONS (contd.)

DAY 5 *Galatians 1:16-17.*
a) Trace Paul's movements after his conversion? Does what he says contradict with Luke's account in Acts 9:18-20?

b) What specific point is Paul seeking to press home in these verses?

DAY 6 *Galatians 1:18-19.*
a) How long did Paul live in seclusion?

b) Is Paul saying here that he got all his knowledge from the other apostles, or from God during his days in the Arabian Desert?

DAY 7 *Galatians 1:20-24; 1 Timothy 1:16.*
a) What dramatic change had taken place in Paul's life?

b) Galatians 1:8,16, 23. What is Paul said to have preached in each of these verses? Can you link them together in a sentence?

NOTES

Revelation

This means the unveiling of something hidden. Biblical revelation is God the Creator disclosing Himself to us: His nature, character, will, ways and plans. When God reveals spiritual truth He expects us to believe it and act upon it. His revelation comes through His word as the Holy Spirit applies its truth to us (John 16:13-15; I Cor. 2:9-11). Christ is the embodiment of God to us, and it is through Christ that God unfolds His wonderful plan of salvation.

Play Actors

The Pharisees were the religious leaders of the Jewish nation in Paul's day. They adhered strictly to their book of rules, the Torah, which then contained 613 written laws. Scripture says of the Pharisees that they were blind to their own faults (Matt. 7:5), to God's working (Luke 12:56), to a true sense of values (Luke 13:15), that they over evaluated tradition (Matt. 15:3-6), were ignorant of God's demands (Matt. 23:14-29) and loved display (Matt. 6:2-16). Jesus, the only one who can see into a man's heart, called them 'hypocrites'. The old Greek meaning for this word was 'play actor'.

Paul, though a Pharisee, was no play actor. He was genuinely out for God's glory and zealously guarded the Jewish religion. But he was SINCERELY wrong. Only a REVELATION from God could have changed Paul. That is exactly what happened (Acts 9:3-9). After that experience on the Damascus Road Paul was transformed from a PERSECUTOR to a PROPAGATOR of the Christian faith.

Called

Paul's experience and revelation were so clear that he was unshakeable in his faith and calling. He began immediately to co-operate with God. He takes pains to prove that God alone brought him his salvation and equipped him to serve Him. God was now implementing in Paul's life what He had planned before Paul was born.

Reflections

Paul's calling was twofold. Christ must first be manifest in him, then through him, to the non-Israelites. This same twofold purpose had been God's design for the Israelites. The unbelievers would be convinced of the reality of the God of Israel as they saw evidence of His life in His people (Ezek. 36:22-23). Likewise we are called to be those who effectively reflect the Christ life. I Peter 2:9 reads: 'But you are a chosen people, a royal priesthood, a holy nation, a people belonging to God, that you may declare the praises of him who called you out of the darkness into his wonderful light'.

Can the world see Jesus in you?

Do we live so close to the Lord today
As we pass to and fro in life's busy way
That the world, in us, a likeness can see
Of the man of Calvary?
Can the world see Jesus in me, in you?
Does our love to Him ring true:
Can the world see Jesus in you?.

STUDY 3

NO COMPROMISE ...

QUESTIONS

(If you read Acts chapter 15 in the Living Bible it will help you get a grasp of this study.)

DAY 1   *Acts 9:26-30; Galatians 1:17-18; 2:1, 6-9.*
a) Compare and contrast the reactions of the apostles to Paul on these two visits to Jerusalem after his conversion.

b) Who accompanied Paul on his second visit?

DAY 2   *Galatians 2:2-5; Acts 11:27-30.*
a) Had the apostles summoned Paul to Jerusalem?

b) How does Paul summarise the reason for his visit in verse 5?

DAY 3   *Galatians 2:2-6.*
a) How were the 'sham Christians' attacking Paul's teaching?

b) What was to be inferred from Titus' experience in Jerusalem?

DAY 4   *Galatians 2:6-10.*
a) Compare and contrast Peter and Paul's commission and message.

b) How are James, Peter and John described here?

QUESTIONS (contd.)

c) What was the significance of their shaking Paul's hand?

DAY 5 *Galatians 2:11-14.*
a) Acts 11:1-18. What had Peter learned from his vision and subsequent visit to Caesarea?

b) Why did Paul now have to rebuke him?

DAY 6 *Galatians 2:13-16.*
a) What is emphasised about justification? What does justification mean?

b) What religious practices do some people depend on for salvation today, instead of faith in Jesus Christ?

DAY 7 *Galatians 2:17-21 (read these portions in the Living Bible and other translations).*
a) In what sense was Paul both dead and alive?

b) Take time to reflect on Christ's love and death. Is Jesus as real to you as He was to the Apostle Paul?

Memory Verse: Galatians 2:20.

Was Paul offbeat?

Since he laboured independently of the other apostles, did Paul have a different message? The Judaizers claimed that the Christian leaders at Jerusalem insisted on the Jewish rites as well as faith in Christ for salvation. Paul preached salvation through faith in Christ alone. Was he wrong?

A test case

The Lord used the fact of Paul and Barnabas taking a gift to Jerusalem to alleviate the famine to give him opportunity to talk to the apostles. He took with him living proof of the liberating power of the gospel in the form of Titus, an uncircumcised Gentile convert. The apostles had been sceptical of receiving Paul as one of them on his first visit (Acts 9:26-30), but this time he was accepted as a dear friend (Acts 15:1-25). Titus also was welcomed as a fellow Christian with no question of him being circumcised! The apostles clearly stood with Paul (Acts 15) and further confirmed that they all preached the same gospel of salvation through faith in Christ alone. James, Peter and John shook hands with Paul, showing they identified fully with him in his teaching and emphasised again that God's commission to Paul was to the Gentile world, and to them, the Jews. (This symbolism of 'identification' in faith and doctrine is still used today in some churches when new members are welcomed and given 'the right hand of fellowship'.)

Straight talk

Imagine Paul having to rebuke Peter openly! Peter had been shown by God (Acts 10:9-20) that Jew and Gentile alike were set free from sin and the law through the liberating gospel. He fellowshipped freely with Gentile converts. However, when the Judaizers turned on the heat of censure, Peter quietly backtracked from this position and showed himself to be inconsistent by not eating with them (this possibly included not 'breaking bread' with them at the Lord's Supper). Peter's attitude affected others adversely (Barnabas in 2:13). Paul's rebuke brought Peter to his senses and put the record straight.

The heart of the gospel

Galatians 2:20 is one of the most important verses in the Bible. It is so important that we will devote our last study in this series to it and its related teachings. Paul was ever forthright. When he said, 'For to me, to LIVE IS CHRIST' (Phil. 1:21) he really meant it. If we could reach heaven by our good works or moral standards, why did Christ die?

The Saviour did not live – He dies;
But in His death was life ...
For we, being crucified with Him
Find life ... forever more.

Paraphrased from A Man Must Live by C. Gilman.

STUDY 4
FAITH INHERITS

QUESTIONS

DAY 1 *Galatians 3:1-3; 1 Corinthians 1:18-25; 2:2.*
a) What newspaper headlines might have been used to describe Paul's reaction to the news he had heard about the Galatians?

b) Why was preaching the cross of Christ so important to Paul?

DAY 2 *Galatians 3:2-5; Ephesians 1:13-14.*
a) How is the experience of becoming a Christian described?

b) What evidence is there that becoming a Christian is sometimes not an easy step to take?

DAY 3 *Galatians 3:1-5.*
a) After beginning well, what mistake were the Galatians now making?

b) What evidence in these verses do we have of the doctrine of the Trinity?

DAY 4 *Galatians 3:6-9; Genesis 15:5-6.*
a) How was Abraham made righteous before God?

b) Those who have faith are said to be what?

QUESTIONS (contd.)

DAY 5 *Galatians 3:10-12; Deuteronomy 27:26; Habakkuk 2:4.*
a) What serious problem arises if we try to keep the law in order to earn salvation?

b) What value does Paul put upon the Old Testament?

DAY 6 *Galatians 3:13-14; Deuteronomy 21:23; I Peter 1:18-19.*
a) Why is the Lord Jesus able to redeem us?

b) What word links Christ's redemptive work and the gift of the Holy Spirit for every believer (v. 14)?

DAY 7 *Galatians 3:14-18; Genesis 22:18.*
a) Who does Paul say will bring blessing to every nation?

b) What could the law not do to this promise of blessing?

Memory Verse: Galatians 3:22.

NOTES

Had we been able to eavesdrop on a conversation between Paul and the Galatians at this time we would have heard something like this:

Paul: What's been happening to you since I last saw you?

Galatians: Oh, we've been learning. The Judaizers have brought us to see we need to be circumcised and keep the Jewish law in order to be Christians.

Paul: How could you be so gullible? You've really been hoodwinked.

Galatians: Sounds all right to us. If God gave laws He must want us to keep them.

Paul: My dear foolish children! Why don't you think? Was it the law that saved you? Didn't the Holy Spirit bring you life when you put your trust in the Saviour?

Galatians: That's right, we didn't know the law. We saw from your teaching that Jesus died to save us from sin.

Paul: Well, if you were saved through faith do you think that you are going to attain spiritual maturity by resorting to legalism?

Galatians: Of course, the Judaizers say that Abraham pleased God by being circumcised and keeping the law, so we have to do the same.

Paul: Nonsense. Abraham was justified by faith (Gen. 15:1-6). It was fourteen years after God declared him righteous before he was circumcised (Gen. 17:23-24) and that was purely to confirm God's covenant (Gen. 12:1-3) and make a distinction between the Israelites and their pagan neighbours. As for the law, that wasn't given until the day of Moses nearly four centuries later!

Galatians: Well, looks like we're wrong about the law. Why on earth did God give it then?

Paul: If a person breaks any part of the law, the penalty is death (Deut. 27:26).

We all find out sooner or later that it is impossible not to break the law. It is then that we realise someone has to get us out of the dilemma or we must suffer God's righteous punishment (Ezek. 18:4).

Galatians: So that's why Jesus died! You said He took the curse for us, bore our sin, and died in our place, that we might be made righteous (2 Cor. 5:21). How could we have been so deluded?

The Galatians had indeed been gullible!

Watch! There are many things today that will cause us to fall into the same trap. Remember, salvation comes through faith in Christ alone.

STUDY 5

IS THE LAW USELESS?

QUESTIONS

DAY 1 *Galatians 3:18-20; Acts 7:53; Romans 3:20.*
a) To what does Paul trace the source of God's dealings with Abraham?

b) Compare and contrast how the law and the promise were both given.

DAY 2 *Galatians 3:18-21.*
a) What purpose is stated for the giving of the law?

b) Can you put into your own words the last sentence in verse 21?

DAY 3 *Galatians 3:22-23; Romans 3:23-24.*
a) To what are we all in bondage?

b) What is the key to our freedom?

DAY 4 *Galatians 3:24-25.*
a) What specific function of the law is highlighted here? How does this link in with the answer to Day 2 a) above?

b) What happens when faith comes?

QUESTIONS (contd.)

DAY 5 *Galatians 3:26; John 1:12-13; Romans 8:16-17.*
a) To what does Paul now link faith?

b) What is emphasised about this new relationship in the 'John' reference?

DAY 6 *Galatians 3:26-27.*
a) As well as being 'sons', what other words are used to describe a Christian's new, close relationship with Jesus Christ?

b) Can you think of any other word that might sum up this new relationship with Christ?

DAY 7 *Galatians 3:28-29.*
a) What does Paul say about Christian unity? What barriers between Christians does being 'in Christ' break down?

b) Share together some of the joys and privileges of being 'heirs' of God's promise.

Memory Verse: Galatians 5:1

NOTES

Paul states quite clearly that the *promise* is superior to the *law*. The promise was given direct to Abraham from God (Gal. 3:18; Gen. 12:1-3); the law was given by a mediator, Moses (Gal. 3:19; Exod. 20). Also the *law* was added to the *promise* (Gal. 3:19).

Why?

Because of sin (v. 19). The New English Bible says: 'It was added to make wrongdoing a legal offence'.

The inference here is that the *law* had a job to do until the One would come through whom the *promise* would be fulfilled. Thus we see that the *law* was only for a limited time, while the *promise* is forever.

The Law and God

God is Holy and desires a Holy people (Lev. 11:44).

The Law is Holy and Perfect and therefore to be perfectly kept (Rom. 7:12).

The Law and Me

The Law reveals God's standards to me (Exod. 20; Rom. 4:15).

The Law reveals that I cannot keep those standards (Rom. 3:20-23).

The Law reveals that I am worthy of death (Deut. 27:26).

The Law and the Promise

The Law *proves* we are all sinners by nature. We are not sinners because we break the law. We break the law because we are sinners!

The Law is *good* and not against God's promise (Gal. 3:21).

The Law effectively *scares* me out of my self-righteous complacency and holds me prisoner in my sin.

The Law *leads* me to cry: 'What must I do to be saved?'

The Law therefore *directs* me to Christ and the eternal promise of eternal salvation from self and sin.

But – the Law is powerless to pardon, so here its function ceases. If we clinch God's promise by faith we are no more prisoners of the law; we are set free in Christ. 'Christ is the end of the law so that there may be righteousness for everyone who believes' (Rom. 10:4).

A wonderful new Relationship

Away back in Genesis when sin separated Adam and Eve from God, they stood naked, as it were, and powerless to cover their shame and transgression. God in compassion took an animal and sacrificed it, using the skin to cover their shame (Gen. 3:21). His yearning heart of love planned to provide an eternal sacrifice for all our sins (Rev. 13:8). The Lamb of God has now been sacrificed, and as we enter into a faith-union with Him (Rom. 6:11), our naked sinfulness is fully covered with Christ our Robe of Righteousness (Isa. 61:10); we have put on Christ (Gal. 3:27).

A wonderful new Family
If we are *in Christ,* there are no barriers. We are *one* in *Him* (Gal. 3:28). Through faith we have inherited the blessings promised to Abraham. We are all in one family – the *faith family* irrespective of colour, nationality, class, etc.

A wonderful new Service
Because Christ has made us His own we do not have to do good to attain, we do not have 'to conform to the law'. We have a desire to cooperate with Him in what He has planned. (Eph. 2:10).

'For when we lived according to our human nature, the sinful desires stirred up by the Law were at work in our bodies, and we were useful in the service of death.

Now, however, we are free from the Law, because we died to that which once held us prisoners. No longer do we serve in the old way of a written law,

But in the new way of the Spirit.' Romans 7:5-6 (Good News Bible)

STUDY 6

SERVANT OR SON?

QUESTIONS

DAY 1 *Galatians 4:1-3.*
a) What 'rights' has a child-heir got? To whom is he subject?

b) What can hold us as slaves (v. 3)?

DAY 2 *Galatians 4:4-5; Philippians 2:6-8.*
a) How does verse 4 tell us that Jesus was both human and divine?

b) What two things did His coming make possible for us?

DAY 3 *Galatians 4:6-7; Romans 8:16-17.*
a) What privileges of sonship are highlighted in these verses?

b) What does Romans 8:16 tell us the Holy Spirit does for us?

DAY 4 *Galatians 4:8-11; Colossians 2:8.*
a) How are the Galatians described before they became Christians?

b) John 17:3. How did Jesus define eternal life?

c) What was Paul's great fear for the Galatians?

QUESTIONS (contd.)

DAY 5   *Galatians 4:12-14.*
a) What good had God brought out of Paul's illness? What might have caused this illness (Acts 14:19; 2 Tim. 3:11)?

b) How had the Galatians reacted to Paul's condition?

DAY 6   *Galatians 4:15-17.*
a) How had the Galatians' attitude to Paul changed?

b) What had caused this change in attitude?

DAY 7   *Galatians 4:18-20; 1 Corinthians 4:15.*
a) What image does Paul use to express his deep concern for them?

b) What lessons can we learn from Paul on how to help someone who is not living as he or she should as a Christian?

Memory Verse: Galatians 5:13-14.

NOTES

Paul uses two illustrations from life situations with which his contemporaries would be familiar.

1. If a child is left an estate by his father, he *potentially* possesses but does not *actually possess* it right away. Until he gets to the age set by his father or the state, he is little better off than a slave. His guardians and trustees manage his personal and legal affairs till he is of age.

Paul draws the comparison that neither Gentiles nor Jews were any better off than slaves. They were alike in bondage to elementary religious practices (v. 3), the one to paganism, the other to the law.

2. It was not uncommon for a wealthy, childless man to legally adopt a slave to become his son and heir. Paul is aware that Christians are sons of God by rebirth (John 1:12-13) but he wishes to use the allegory here of being brought from slavery to sonship (Rom. 8:15-16).

God's *plan* to accomplish this was put into operation at His chosen time (v. 4). The *person* ordained was His Divine Son and Equal (John 5:18). The *pattern* was that Christ would become man (John 1:14) in order to identify with us and redeem us (Heb. 4:15; John 1:29). Through Christ, believers are adopted into the family of God.

Will you revert to slavery?
The Galatians are known of God (v. 9) and have had their eyes opened to the truth of salvation through faith in Christ. Now they are allowing themselves to be tricked by the legalistic teachers into bondage again, not the bondage of paganism, but of the law. What foolishness! Surely they should know better! Read 1 Timothy 4:1-4 and earnestly pray that we will not fall into the same error.

Please listen to me!
Paul pleads in love: 'I've had to write pretty straight to you. You once so wholeheartedly embraced the truth, accepting me when I was in a pitiful condition.

You were so blessed you would have given your right hand for me. Why do you turn away now? How I wish I could talk face to face with you. You don't understand how much I long to see you established and mature in Christ. My agony of soul is almost more than I can bear ...'.

STUDY 7

THE GOAL OF THE GOSPEL

QUESTIONS

DAY 1   *Galatians 4:21-23; Genesis 16:1-4, 15-16; 21:1-5; Romans 4:18-21.*
a) Who were these two sons of Abraham Paul refers to?

b) Which son was born as a result of God's promise? Why was his birth special?

DAY 2   *Galatians 4:24-27.*
a) What is said about the children of each mother?

b) To what family did Paul say the believers really belonged? Why is this a large family (Acts 28:28; Rom. 9:25-26)?

DAY 3   *Galatians 4:28-31; Genesis 21:9-10.*
a) Why is Isaac used to represent believers?

b) Who alone can enjoy God's inheritance? (Which family are you in?)

DAY 4   *Galatians 5:1; Romans 8:1-4.*
a) How is our freedom achieved (Lev. 26:13)?

b) Should we take this freedom for granted?

QUESTIONS (contd.)

DAY 5 *Galatians 5:2-6.*
a) What particular form of bondage or slavery does Paul warn against here?

b) How does verse 6 link in with James 1:14-20?

DAY 6 *Galatians 5:7-12; Matthew 23:13-19.*
a) What is the Christian life compared to? What other illustration does Paul use?

b) What appeared to be adding to the Galatians' confusion (v. 11)?

DAY 7 *Galatians 5:7-12.*
a) What had the Galatians been obeying (v. 7)? What had the Lord Jesus said about Himself (John 14:6)?

b) What does Paul say about those who promote error?

Memory Verse: Galatians 5:16.

NOTES

These two lists summarise pretty clearly verses 21-31. Surely as we look down the list we must be challenged to seek to co-operate with God in His divine purposes in and through us.

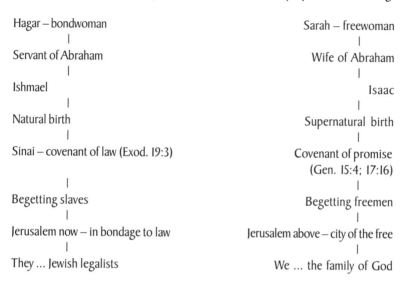

Hagar – bondwoman | Sarah – freewoman
Servant of Abraham | Wife of Abraham
Ishmael | Isaac
Natural birth | Supernatural birth
Sinai – covenant of law (Exod. 19:3) | Covenant of promise (Gen. 15:4; 17:16)
Begetting slaves | Begetting freemen
Jerusalem now – in bondage to law | Jerusalem above – city of the free
They ... Jewish legalists | We ... the family of God

Abraham and Sarah's attempt to help God out with His work is still having far-reaching effects today. This poem was written about the six-day war in 1967 when Ishmael's descendants (Arab nation) and Isaac's descendants (Israel) were in bitter conflict. It is another commentary on human nature and the folly of scheming instead of trusting.

First-born but dispossessed, now Ishmael stands
Angry and militant astride the shifting sand
Surrounding Aqaba: And swears he will wage a holy war.
Unmindful of the fact that in this age or any other,
Isaac still is truly apt to be the chosen one.
The years of ceaseless wandering, sweat and dust and deprivation
Have increased his lust for vengeance.
Hagar's tears keep fresh the seeds of hatred
Ishmael hears again the ancient edict, and he burns.
By all that's holy this is the time he'll show

That upstart sibling Isaac where to go.
In Israel the wily Isaac waits, feigns innocence
But secretly determines; now's his chance to lash out.
Is not he the favoured son?
His is the land of promise. He will see it stays so.
Abraham turns in his grave and murmurs:
'Would to God I'd known ... I could have waited.'

Which side are you on? If you are truly a child of 'promise' make sure you stay free in the freedom Christ has provided (Gal. 5:1), for the goal of the gospel is to set us free and to keep us free from all that would keep us from enjoying our inheritance in Christ.

STUDY 8

LOVE FULFILS THE LAW

QUESTIONS

DAY 1 *Galatians 5:13; John 8:32,36.*
a) What has Paul been saying believers are freed from?

b) How are those who are free to behave?

DAY 2 *Galatians 5:14-15; Leviticus 19:18; Romans 13:8-10.*
a) What does it take for a church to self-destruct?

b) How will others know that we love our neighbour as ourselves? How is it possible for a Christian to love like this (Rom. 5:5)?

DAY 3 *Galatians 5:16-18, 24-25.*
a) What has Paul already said about the Holy Spirit in this letter (3:3; 4:6)? What does he say now?

b) What picture does Paul use to indicate that a Christian's behaviour before and after conversion is to be radically different (v. 24).

DAY 4 *Galatians 5:16-17.*
a) What standard of behaviour is set for the Christian in I Peter 1:14-15?

QUESTIONS (contd.)

b) Why can Paul say that this standard is possible for a Christian?

DAY 5 *Galatians 5:16-18, 25-26.*
a) Discuss some of the practical ways in which the Holy Spirit can help a Christian lead a holy life.

b) What is suggested by the following verses: Ephesians 6:17-18; Matthew 4:10-11?

DAY 6 *Galatians 5:19-21.*
a) List the sins mentioned under the following headings and then discuss how they might manifest themselves today:

   1) Sexual sins

   2) Pagan practices

   3) Sins of passion

   4) Sins of indulgence

b) What warning is given to people who live like this?

DAY 7 *Galatians 5:22-26.*
a) What does the Holy Spirit produce in the lives of God's children?

b) How are we to live with regard to the Holy Spirit?

NOTES

From Death to Life
In Galatians chapters 3 and 4 Paul has established six things that God's plan of salvation accomplishes:

1) We are LIBERATED from subservience to the law (Gal. 3:13, 22-25; 4:1,21-31).
2) We are LIBERATED from the curse of the law (Gal. 3:13, 24).
3) We are LIBERATED from the law's inability to make us righteous (Gal. 3:21; Rom. 8:3).
4) We are LIBERATED from the death sentence the law had served on us (2 Cor. 3:6-8).
5) We are LIBERATED by the Spirit of God (2 Cor. 3:6, 17).
6) We are LIBERATED by the death and resurrection of Christ into glorious eternal life and freedom (Gal. 2:19, 20; 3:2; 4:6; Rom. 7:4).

Stand fast in this FREEDOM
In Galatians 5:1-4 Paul says: 'Now you have been made completely free in Christ, see that you continue to stand in this freedom. Don't get trapped into legalism.

Although the law still stands it has no longer a claim upon those who are in Christ' (Gal. 5:14; Rom. 8:4).

Don't use this FREEDOM as an excuse to indulge your physical desires
The sinful nature or flesh (that is what I am by nature) always wants to do its own thing! Christ hasn't called us to do our own thing. He has freed us for loving service.

One of the clearest illustrations of this in Scripture is the picture of the bond-slave who loves his master and chooses to serve him rather than accept the freedom which is his due. He returns to his master's house to serve exactly as he used to do, but now it is not a case of 'I must because I have to', but rather 'I will because I love my master and freely choose to'. It is now a service of love (Exod. 21:2-6).

Love fulfils the Law
Paul has shown that the law is impotent to make us righteous and has established our complete inability to keep its demands and thus meet God's requirements. No, he says, there is a way ... it is the way of love.

Galatians 5:13 could be written as an equation:

LIBERTY – love = license (indulging the sinful nature, enslavement to sin)
LIBERTY + love = service (self-giving)

The Levitical law demanded 'love your neighbour as yourself' (Lev. 19:18) but as those 'who walked after the flesh' (i.e. independently of God) we could not fulfil it.

Now that same commandment (Gal. 5:14), coming to those who 'live by the Spirit' (v. 16) can be kept 'because God has poured out his love into our hearts by the Holy Spirit' (Rom. 5:5). 'Love is the fulfilling of the law' (Rom. 13:10, AV).

God's demands are fully met in Christ (see Rom. 8:4; 13:8-10; Heb. 10:5- 10.)

Note too that Galatians 5:13 says we are to serve one another in LOVE. Love always issues in self-giving.

GOD is self-giving. In LOVE He gave Himself in His Son to bring us to Sonship (John 3:16).
CHRIST is self-giving. IN LOVE He implemented the Father's will at Calvary (Gal. 2:20).
WE are to be self-giving. In LOVE we are to serve one another (Gal. 5:13).

Paul says in I Corinthians 13:13 that love is the greatest! Read through that whole chapter to see how futile are all our 'good works' if LOVE is not the motivating factor.

Two lifestyles

How effectively these are contrasted! We would all like to skip swiftly over the gruesome list in verses 19-21 saying 'I'm not as bad as all that'. If we live according to the sinful nature then we can only produce the 'works of the flesh' (5:19, AV).

If we produce the works of the flesh we must pay the penalty (Jas. 1:14,15).

Take note that with God there are no degrees of sin. Hate (and not to love is hate!) is murder in embryo (Matt. 15:19). Lustful looking is equal to adultery (Matt. 5:28). Those who habitually do these things will never enter the kingdom of God (Gal. 5:21). Are any of us candidates for this lifestyle?

The Spirit, on the other hand, produces a harvest of good things in the life of the believer. Verses 22-23 correspond with I Corinthians 13:4-6. Only the Spirit of God can produce a Christlike life; and there can be no law against Christ-likeness!

To head the list is the word 'Love' again, bringing us back to I Corinthians 13.

God made no mistake when He gave us the New Commandment. For love is the fulfilling of the law.

A new command I give you:
Love one another.
As I have loved you,
So you must love one another' (John 13:34).

STUDY 9

DYING TO LIVE

QUESTIONS

DAY 1   *Galatians 6:1-3; 5:22-23; I Peter 4:8.*
a) What does Paul say should be done for others? What needs to be avoided?

b) Which fruit of the Spirit is required to do all this?

DAY 2   *Galatians 6:2-5,10; John 13:34-35.*
a) What could be another way of saying 'the law of Christ' (v. 2)?

b) Is it possible to think that we are more spiritual than we really are? How can any inconsistency be avoided?

DAY 3   *Galatians 6:6; Romans 15:27; I Corinthians 9:11-12.*
a) Read verse 6 in several versions and then write it in your own words.

b) Which fruit of the Spirit is exercised in such a ministry?

DAY 4   *Galatians 6:7-8; Romans 6:19-23; I John 2:15-17.*
a) What natural principle is also related to spiritual growth?

b) From what comes a harvest of holiness? Discuss practical steps we can take to 'sow' correctly.

QUESTIONS (contd.)

DAY 5   *Galatians 6:9-10; Hebrews 12:3-5.*
a) What kind of things can make us 'weary in doing good'?

b) How does Paul encourage us to persevere?

DAY 6   *Galatians 6:11-13; Look also at Galatians 4:14-15.*
a) Can you think of two reasons why Paul might write these last verses in his own handwriting and in big print?

b) What two less than worthy motives prompted the Judaizers to 'deceive' the Galatians?

DAY 7   *Galatians 6:14-18.*
a) Why does Paul boast (glory) alone in the cross?

b) What 'rule' does Paul refer to in verse 16 (2 Cor. 5:17)?

NOTES

It's dying, not doing!

Has Paul convinced you that salvation comes, not by anything you do, but by what Christ has done? Only in Christ can we die out to sin, self-centredness and independence of God. When our lives become Christ-centred and we live by the rule of love, the law is fulfilled.

Everything new!

Think of a caterpillar going through its physical metamorphosis. It casts off its old life (which kept it subject to the law of gravity) and soars away on its wings of freedom (the law of aerodynamics has taken over). The old law still exists and will certainly come into play if the butterfly doesn't use its new equipment.

For the Christian a spiritual metamorphosis has taken place. Outside of Christ I was subject to and condemned by the law. In Christ I soar away free because the law of the Spirit of Life has taken over. I am a NEW PERSON, utterly free from the law of sin and death. Search the Scriptures for all that belongs to our NEW LIFE. Here are a few references to help you:

New Birth: John 3:3,6; I Peter 1:23; New Babe: I Peter 2:2.
New Name: Revelation 2:17; 3:12. New Way: Hebrews 10:20.
New Man: Ephesians 4:24; Colossians 3:10.
Everything New: Revelation 21:5.

Legalist or lover?

Paul affirms that the legalists are braggarts (vv. 12-13) compromisers (v. 12) persuaders (v. 12) hypocrites (v. 13). Beware! We too can all fall into false pride, compromise, self-righteousness. The only antidote to all of these is life in the Spirit, the way of love (Gal. 5:13-14). Read Galatians 6:1-2, 6, 10 again. Love restores the fallen, stays the weak, cares for God's children, provides fellowship for fellow Christians and a ministry of life to all men.

PERSPECTIVE ON GLORY

Paul exposes the falseness of the Judaizer's teaching. If they persuade the Gentiles that circumcision, as well as faith in Christ, is necessary for salvation, they will have won their point. They will be able to boast, pat themselves on the back as it were, that they have won Jewish converts. The danger of self-glory is in sharp contrast here to Paul's own outlook. Paul's boasting was in the cross of Christ alone. He magnified the PERSON of the cross: Christ. He knew the POWER of the cross: his own changed life. He experienced the LIBERTY of the cross: deliverance from self-centredness (Gal. 2:20), the sinful nature or flesh (Gal. 5:24) and the world (Gal. 6:14). He realised the PURPOSE of the cross: a new creation (Gal. 6:15) and a New Israel of God (Gal. 6:16).

STUDY 10

IT'S ALL IN OUR UNION WITH CHRIST

QUESTIONS

DAY 1 *Galatians 2:16-17; 3:8, 11, 13, 14; 5:4.*
What two key words beginning with the letters j and r does Paul use to describe the experience of becoming a Christian? Try and describe what these words mean.

DAY 2 *Romans 16:7; 1 Corinthians 1:30; Galatians 3:28; Philippians 1:1; Colossians 1:2.*
a) How are believers described in these verses?

b) What happens as a result of this (2 Cor. 5:17)?

DAY 3 *Galatians 2:20; Romans 6:1-7.*
a) What is the immediate consequence of union with Christ?

b) What is this followed by?

DAY 4 *Romans 6:11-18.*
a) How is sin affected by our union with Christ?

b) What are we to do with our body?

QUESTIONS (contd.)

DAY 5   *Galatians 2:20-21; 5:25.*
a) What does Paul say about his 'living' as a Christian in these verses?

b) Why is the Holy Spirit important in a Christian's life (John 15:26; Rom. 8:9-16, 26)?

DAY 6   *Galatians 5:16-17, 24-26.*
a) What tension is highlighted in these verses?

b) How are we to relate to the Holy Spirit in order to be holy?

DAY 7   *Galatians 2:20-21.*
What teaching has impressed you the most from a study of this letter?

NOTES

What happened at the Cross?

If you say 'Christ died for my sin', you are right – but this isn't the whole answer. There is another aspect of the Cross. Colossians 3:1-3 says that WE died and rose with Christ. Paul prayed in Philippians 3 that he might have an identification with Christ in His resurrection and a conformity to His death. Romans 6 talks about us being co-buried (v. 4), co-joined (v. 5) and co-crucified (v. 6) with Christ. What does this mean in practical experience? It just means we are to have a realistic grasp of this new, radical IN-CHRIST relationship.

The Scriptures we have studied this week talk of a new STATUS through our new RELATIONSHIP. When we understand the power and authority of our new status we go on to experience the reality of our new state.

Being IN-CHRIST means I have *died* out to the evil status of bondage to Satan and I have *come alive* in a new relationship and, because of *the person I am now in partnership with*, I have release, freedom and the ability to cope with temptation, etc.

There is no ground here for doubt or argument. The Scriptures clearly state a FACT, we ARE IN A NEW RELATIONSHIP! James Verney says: 'The experience in which a man becomes right with God through faith in Christ is the experience whereby he became a DEAD MAN, so far as sin is concerned, and a LIVING MAN so far as God is concerned. As long as faith is at normal tension the life of sin is inconceivable.'

The Cross and the law

Romans 6 teaches that in Christ we have died out to sin. Romans 7 says we are also dead so far as the law is concerned. We now see it is futile 'trying to be good', trying to reach God's perfect standard (the law) by self effort. Instead, holiness of life is produced in us on the resources of our new relationship. 'I am strengthened for everything in the strengthening Christ' (Phil. 4:13).

The Cross and the old 'me'

Romans 8 teaches that we are delivered from the flesh, that is the old self which acted independently of God. Even if our intentions are 'good' if we act in our own strength and righteousness instead of reliance on Christ within, God cannot bless or condone our actions. This principle of 'Union life in Christ' sets me free from 'death-producing' independence.

God's great plan is to make us indwelt agents of His Divine life. That's what Paul means when he says 'I have been crucified with Christ' (The old me? That's finished.) 'Nevertheless I live' (of course I'm not physically dead), 'Yet not I, but Christ liveth in me' (I'm no longer an independent, self-orientated person for Christ's very life is in me); 'And the life which I now live in the flesh (as I go on as a human being in this earthly scene) I live by the faith of the Son of God' (I operate now on the basis of total reliance on an indwelling Christ) 'who loved me and gave Himself for me'. (Whose very coming and living and dying was for this very purpose of REALISED UNION.)

ANSWER GUIDE

The following pages contain an Answer Guide. It is recommended that answers to the questions be attempted before turning to this guide. It is only a guide and the answers given should not be treated as exhaustive.

GUIDE TO INTRODUCTORY STUDY

'TRADITION OR TRUTH?'

Select seven members of your group who could take the various roles in the playlet and read their portions clearly and confidently. Make sure they have the material beforehand so that they can become familiar with the text.

After the play either read together or have a member read Philippians 3:2-5 from the Living or Good News Bible.

Now look up the references given in the section 'About Galatians'. If there is not enough time to read all the portions, then explain it briefly in your own words (you will have prepared it beforehand!) and encourage everyone to go over the references at home.

Instruct them to start on their questions for the next study, making sure they prepare the allotted amount each day.

These studies have been prepared using the New International Version of the Bible, but members are encouraged to use and/or refer to as many other translations as possible to help them understand the text.

GUIDE TO STUDY 1

DAY 1 a) Paul.
b) As an apostle.
c) To the churches in Galatia (v. 2).
d) To warn the Galatians against being turned aside from the truth of the gospel.

DAY 2 a) That he was a true apostle and thus spoke with God's authority.
b) The resurrection of Jesus Christ.

DAY 3 a) They had the same heavenly Father (NIV has 'our Father', v. 3); they both needed the Lord Jesus to rescue them from their sins.
b) Grace is described as the undeserved favour of God – He need not have reached down to save us, but He did.
Peace is the result of a cleansed conscience and the knowledge that we can live in harmony with God.

DAY 4 a) He died for us; it was a deliberate choice on His part.
b) It was substitutionary ('for our sins') and was willed by God; it brought about a rescue from an evil world system.

DAY 5 a) No; we can only receive salvation through faith in Christ's sacrifice to save us.
b) He instinctively began to give praise and glory to God.

DAY 6 a) The gospel of Christ. Paul was adamant that there was only one true gospel.
b) They were being led into confusion as to what was the true gospel and as a result were deserting 'the gospel of Christ'.

DAY 7 a) This would indicate that he was pleasing God by insisting that the true gospel be preached. It would also suggest that those who were opposing the true gospel were doing it for personal motives and thus their teaching should be rejected (4:17).
b) At the heart of the gospel is the death, burial and resurrection of Jesus Christ.

Note: If there is time after the study it might be good to discuss areas where people are mistaken in their concepts of salvation, i.e. the fallacy of doing good in order to merit salvation, etc.

GALATIANS • ANSWER GUIDE

• • • • •

49

GUIDE TO STUDY 2

DAY 1   a) It has no human origin.
b) The gospel had been clearly revealed to him by Jesus Christ. Peter's grasp of spiritual truth had also been directly divinely inspired.

DAY 2   a) An all-out, devout, law-abiding Jew who by virtue of his training and education and spiritual standing had much to be proud of.
b) To persecute the followers of Christ whom he felt were sincerely misguided in their beliefs.

DAY 3   a) To the grace of God.
b) To preach the gospel among the Gentiles. He responded immediately with complete obedience.

DAY 4   a) Yes. He preached about a Person, the Lord Jesus ('preach him', v. 16).
b) No; he was constantly overwhelmed by Jesus' love, grace and forgiveness shown to him.

DAY 5   a) He went to Arabia and later returned to Damascus. No; just because Luke does not mention the visit to Arabia does not mean that it did not take place.
b) He was no second-rate apostle who needed to go to Jerusalem to have apostleship conferred on him. He was an apostle appointed by God and hence what he preached was of divine origin.

DAY 6   a) Three years.
b) He emphasises that all he taught was given him by God and it had not come 'second-hand' from men.

DAY 7   a) He was now a propagator and not a persecutor of the Christian faith.
b) A 'gospel'; 'his Son'; 'the faith'.
Personal. The Christian faith is good news (gospel) about a Person; it is not a set of rules or regulations.

GUIDE TO STUDY 3

DAY 1   a) They were at first afraid to identify with him and uncertain of his position as a Christian, but later accepted him as one of themselves and agreed with his teaching.
b) At least Barnabas and Titus.

DAY 2   a) No; he and Barnabas were taking the gift from the church in Antioch to Judea to help them in the time of famine prophesied by Agabus.
b) He went in defence of the 'truth of the gospel'.

DAY 3   a) They maintained that the Gentiles really must conform to all the old Jewish rites (such as circumcision) to be saved.
b) That if circumcision had been really necessary for salvation then Titus would have been asked to be circumcised, which he was not.

DAY 4   a) Both had been commissioned and blessed by God; they both preached the same gospel, Peter to the Jews, Paul to the Gentiles.
b) As pillars or leaders.
c) It symbolised their full identification with him in his faith and ministry.

DAY 5   a) That God's grace now extended as freely to the Gentiles as to the Jews; thus, by conversion Jews and Gentiles were one in the Lord.
b) By back-tracking from what God had revealed to him, Peter was showing himself to be inconsistent in his behaviour.

DAY 6   a) It is only possible through faith in Jesus Christ alone and it has nothing to do with keeping the law.
Justification is God's declaration that the guilty sinner is righteous on the basis of Christ's sacrifice.
b) Personal. Some suggestions will include: church going, charitable giving, trying to help others, etc.

DAY 7   a) He was dead to his former life as a religious Jew; he was now alive in his relationship with God through Jesus Christ.
b) Personal.

GALATIANS • ANSWER GUIDE

•
•
•
•
•

(51)

GUIDE TO STUDY 4

DAY 1 a) Shock, horror, disappointment, concern, unbelief, etc.
b) It was at the heart of the gospel and brought salvation from sin.

DAY 2 a) As believing and receiving the Holy Spirit.
b) Paul refers to the Galatians as having suffered.

DAY 3 a) They thought they had to observe the law as part of salvation.
b) God, the Holy Spirit and Jesus Christ are all referred to.

DAY 4 a) He believed God's word spoken to him.
b) Blessed.

DAY 5 a) Failure to observe *all* of the law brings down its 'curse' on us.
b) He quotes freely from it, accepting its authority.

DAY 6 a) He suffered in our place the punishment of our sins; He took upon Himself the curse of the law that was ours.
b) Faith.

DAY 7 a) The Lord Jesus.
b) It could not annul or render this promise from God void.

GUIDE TO STUDY 5

DAY 1
a) To God's grace (v. 18).
b) The law was given third-hand: from God, by angels, through mediator to the people.
The promise was given directly from God to Abraham (Gen. 12:1-3).

DAY 2
a) To make us conscious of sin and see this as a violation of God's holy law.
b) If the law had been able to confer spiritual life then our justification (right standing before God) would have come by the law.

DAY 3
a) To sin and the justice of the law.
b) Faith in Jesus Christ.

DAY 4
a) That of leading us to Christ.
Only when we are made conscious of our sin and the righteous demands of a holy God will we seek salvation in Jesus Christ.
b) We are no longer under the law's supervision.

DAY 5
a) With becoming God's children.
b) It is not linked to any human achievement or pedigree; it is all the supernatural work of God.

DAY 6
a) Being 'clothed' with Christ, 'in Christ', 'Abraham's seed'.
b) The best is possibly faith-union!

DAY 7
a) It is only possible between believers who 'belong to Christ', who are 'one in Christ'.
Barriers of colour, nationality, social class or denomination.
b) Personal; the list is endless: blessings of fellowship, having His word, peace, joy, and a future in heaven, etc.

GUIDE TO STUDY 6

DAY 1 a) The rights of a slave, that is, no rights!
To guardians and trustees set by his father.
b) 'Elementary ideas' (NEB mg), things that are now outdated by Christ.

DAY 2 a) It says He was God's Son, yet born of a woman.
b) Our release from the bondage of the law into the freedom of sonship.

DAY 3 a) God as our Father, access into His presence, an inheritance, a glorious future.
b) He assures us of our sonship; He assures us of our salvation.

DAY 4 a) As being in slavery to false gods and to religious rituals.
b) As knowing God.
c) They were in danger of returning to a certain kind of slavery.

DAY 5 a) It had allowed him to preach the Gospel to the Galatians.
The battering and disfigurement from stoning and physical exhaustion.
b) They did not allow it to come between Paul and his message.

DAY 6 a) They were now treating him as if he was an enemy.
b) 'People' (obviously false teachers) who had deliberately set out to wreck Paul's good relationship and influence with the Galatians so as to introduce their own ideas.

DAY 7 a) He is prepared to suffer the pains of childbirth for them all over again.
b) Affirm what is good, clearly yet gently state the truth, be deeply concerned.

GUIDE TO STUDY 7

DAY 1 a) Ishmael and Isaac.
b) Isaac. He was a miracle of God's grace due to the advanced age of his parents.

DAY 2 a) Hagar's are slaves while Sarah's are free.
b) The heavenly Jerusalem (representing the Christian Church).
Many Gentiles have become believers.

DAY 3 a) They are born (again) in a supernatural manner by the Holy Spirit (John 3:3-6).
b) Only those who are 'free', that is, those who are born-again.

DAY 4 a) Through Jesus Christ.
b) No; we need to be careful to maintain it.

DAY 5 a) That of circumcision.
b) True faith should not be hidden; it should show itself in loving deeds of practical service.

DAY 6 a) A race.
Yeast spreading through a batch of dough.
b) The suggestion that Paul himself was preaching the necessity of circumcision.

DAY 7 a) The truth.
That He was the truth.
b) They will have to face up to the serious consequences of their false teaching (v. 10).

GUIDE TO STUDY 8

DAY 1   a) Depending on the law to obtain salvation.
b) Avoid sin and act in love towards others.

DAY 2   a) A lack of love that leads to infighting.
b) We will be fulfilling the law, not with the intention of trying to earn salvation but as a result of it.
The Holy Spirit implants God's love in a believer.

DAY 3   a) The Spirit initiates salvation; He dwells within a believer.
The Holy Spirit is essential to our sanctification.
b) That of crucifiying the sinful nature.

DAY 4   a) That of holiness.
b) He knows the Holy Spirit is available to help.

DAY 5   Personal. The Holy Spirit can bring Bible verses to our memory which we can use as a sword against the devil; He helps us pray.

DAY 6   a) 1) Immorality, impurity, debauchery.
      2) Idolatry, witchcraft.
      3) Hatred, discord, jealousy, fits of rage, selfish ambition, dissensions, factions, envy.
      4) Drunkenness, orgies.
b) They will not inherit God's kingdom.

DAY 7   a) A harvest of good things which can never be legislated against.
b) We are to keep in step with Him.

GUIDE TO STUDY 9

DAY 1   a) Restoration (if required); mutual sharing of burdens. ('Restore' is used here in the sense of a mason repairing a broken wall or a doctor setting a broken limb.)
Falling into sin ourselves.
b) Love (with its attendant attributes of patience, gentleness, etc.).

DAY 2   a) The law of love.
b) Yes (Paul refers to deception).
By closely examining our lives; by remembering that we are individually responsible before God for our conduct.

DAY 3   a) The person being instructed in the Word should contribute to his teacher's support. (This is God's way of meeting the needs of those who give themselves wholly to the work of God.)
b) Love.

DAY 4   a) Reaping what we sow.
b) Sowing to the Spirit and not sowing to the sinful nature.
Personal; suggestions: avoid bad company, read good literature, etc.

DAY 5   a) Discouragement; disappointment; seeming unanswered prayer; the indifference of others to the Gospel; neglect of prayer (Isa. 40:31).
b) By saying that harvest time will come. (Read I Cor. 2:9-10. As well as blessings now there is much more awaiting us.)

DAY 6   a) Paul may have written in large letters because he had poor eyesight. Or, more likely, he was determined to get his message of salvation through faith alone, by grace, over to the Galatians.
b) To avoid persecution and to have 'converts' to boast about.

DAY 7   a) It alone has brought about a radical change in his life.
b) The principle of being a 'new creation' in Christ.

GALATIANS • ANSWER GUIDE • • • • • • •

GUIDE TO STUDY 10

DAY 1   Being justified and redeemed.
Justification: the guilty sinner is declared righteous before God.
Redemption: the sinner is released from the bondage of sin.

DAY 2   a) As being 'in Christ'.
b) They become part of God's 'new creation'.

DAY 3   a) Death to sin; a radical breach with the world around us.
b) New life in Christ.

DAY 4   a) We no longer need to be dominated by it.
b) We are to offer the parts of our body as instruments to God.

DAY 5   a) Christ lives within; he lives by faith; he lives by the Holy Spirit.
b) He reveals Christ; He controls, gives life, puts sin or the old life to death, gives assurance of salvation, helps in prayer.

DAY 6   a) The sinful nature seeking to oppose our obedience to God.
b) Live by Him; let ourselves be led by Him; keep in step with Him.
(We are to obey the prompting of the Holy Spirit.)

DAY 7   Personal.

THE WORD WORLDWIDE

We first heard of WORD WORLDWIDE over twenty years ago when Marie Dinnen, its founder, shared excitedly about the wonderful way ministry to one needy woman had exploded to touch many lives. It was great to see the Word of God being made central in the lives of thousands of men and women, then to witness the life-changing results of them applying the Word to their circumstances. Over the years the vision for WORD WORLDWIDE has not dimmed in the hearts of those who are involved in this ministry. God is still at work through His Word and in today's self-seeking society, the Word is even more relevant to those who desire true meaning and purpose in life. WORD WORLDWIDE is a ministry of WEC International, an interdenominational missionary society, whose sole purpose is to see Christ known, loved and worshipped by all, particularly those who have yet to hear of His wonderful name. This ministry is a vital part of our work and we warmly recommend the WORD WORLDWIDE 'Geared for Growth' Bible studies to you. We know that as you study His Word you will be enriched in your personal walk with Christ. It is our hope that as you are blessed through these studies, you will find opportunities to help others discover a personal relationship with Jesus. As a mission we would encourage you to work with us to make Christ known to the ends of the earth.

Stewart and Jean Moulds – British Directors, **WEC International**.

A full list of over 50 'Geared for Growth' studies can be obtained from:

John and Ann Edwards
5 Louvaine Terrace, Hetton-le-Hole, Tyne & Wear, DH5 9PP
Tel. 0191 5262803 Email: rhysjohn.edwards@virgin.net

Anne Jenkins
2 Windermere Road, Carnforth, Lancs., LA5 9AR
Tel. 01524 734797 Email: anne@jenkins.abelgratis.com

UK Website: www.gearedforgrowth.co.uk

OLD TESTAMENT

Triumphs Over Failures: A Study in Judges ISBN 1-85792-888-1 (above left)
Messenger of Love: A Study in Malachi ISBN 1-85792-885-7 (above right)
The Beginning of Everything: A Study in Genesis 1-11 ISBN 0-90806-728-3
Hypocrisy in Religion: A Study in Amos ISBN 0-90806-706-2
Unshakeable Confidence: A Study in Habakkuk & Joel ISBN 0-90806-751-8
A Saviour is Promised: A Study in Isaiah 1 - 39 ISBN 0-90806-755-0
Our Magnificent God: A Study in Isaiah 40 - 66 ISBN 1-85792-909-8
The Throne and Temple: A Study in 1 & 2 Chronicles ISBN 1-85792-910-1
The Cost of Obedience: A Study in Jeremiah ISBN 0-90806-761-5
Focus on Faith: A Study of 10 Old Testament Characters ISBN 1-85792-890-3
Faith, Courage and Perserverance: A Study in Ezra ISBN 1-85792-949-7
Amazing Love: A Study in Hosea ISBN 1-84550-004-0

NEW TESTAMENT

The World's Only Hope: A Study in Luke ISBN 1-85792-886-5 (above left)
Walking in Love: A Study in John's Epistles ISBN 1-85792-891-1 (above right)
Faith that Works: A Study in James ISBN 0-90806-701-1
Made Completely New: A Study in Colossians & Philemon ISBN 0-90806-721-6
Jesus-Christ, Who is He? A Study in John's Gospel ISBN 0-90806-716-X
Entering by Faith: A Study in Hebrews ISBN 1-85792-914-4
Heavenly Living: A Study in Ephesians ISBN 1-85792-911-X
The Early Church: A Study in Acts 1-12 ISBN 0-90806-736-4
Worldwide Evangelization: A Study in Acts 13-28 ISBN 1-84550-005-9
Get Ready: A Study in 1 & 2 Thessalonians ISBN 1-85792-948-9
Glimpses of the King: A Study in Matthew's Gospel ISBN 1-84550-007-5
The Drama of Revelation: A Study in Revelation ISBN 1-84550-020-2
Controlled by Love: A Study in 2 Corinthians ISBN 1-84550-022-9
People and Problems in the Church: A Study in 1st Corinthians
ISBN 1-84550-021-0

· · · · ·

CHARACTER

Abraham: A Study of Genesis 12-25 ISBN 1-85792-887-3 (above left)
Serving the Lord: A Study of Joshua ISBN 1-85792-889-X (above right)
Achieving the Impossible: A Study of Nehemiah ISBN 0-90806-707-0
God plans for Good: A Study of Joseph ISBN 0-90806-700-3
A Man After God's Own Heart: A Study of David ISBN 0-90806-746-1
Grace & Grit: A Study of Ruth & Esther ISBN 1-85792-908-X
Men of Courage: A Study of Elijah & Elisha ISBN 1-85792-913-6
Meek but Mighty: A Study of Moses ISBN 1-85792-951-9
Highly Esteemed: A Study of Daniel ISBN 1-84550-006-7
A Man with a Choice: A Study in the Life of Solomon ISBN 1-84550-023-7
God Cares: A Study in the Life of Jonah ISBN 1-84550-024-5
The Man God Chose: A Study in the Life of Jacob ISBN 1-84550-025-3

THEMES

God's Heart, My Heart: World Mission ISBN 1-85792-892-X (above left)
Freedom: You Can Find it! ISBN 0-90806-702-X (above right)
Freely Forgiven: A Study in Redemption ISBN 0-90806-720-8
The Problems of Life! Is there an Answer? ISBN 1-85792-907-1
Understanding the Way of Salvation ISBN 0-90082-880-3
Saints in Service: 12 Bible Characters ISBN 1-85792-912-8
Finding Christ in the Old Testament: Pre-existence and Prophecy
ISBN 0-90806-739-9

Christian Focus Publications

publishes books for all ages

Our mission statement –

STAYING FAITHFUL

In dependence upon God we seek to help make His infallible word, the Bible, relevant. Our aim is to ensure that the Lord Jesus Christ is presented as the only hope to obtain forgiveness of sin, live a useful life and look forward to heaven with Him.

REACHING OUT

Christ's last command requires us to reach out to our world with His gospel. We seek to help fulfil that by publishing books that point people towards Jesus and help them develop a Christ-like maturity. We aim to equip all levels of readers for life, work, ministry and mission.

Books in our adult range are published in three imprints.

Christian Focus contains popular works including biographies, commentaries, basic doctrine, and Christian living. Our children's books are also published in this imprint.

Mentor focuses on books written at a level suitable for Bible College and seminary students, pastors, and other serious readers; the imprint includes commentaries, doctrinal studies, examination of current issues, and church history.

Christian Heritage contains classic writings from the past.

For details of our titles visit us on our website
www.christianfocus.com

Christian Focus Publications Ltd
Geanies House, Fearn, Tain,
Ross-shire, IV20 ITW, Scotland, United Kingdom.
info@christianfocus.com